WORD RHY'

From the Life of A

To Jasmine
of our Jamaican people
eleanthomas
March 13/86.

WORD RHYTHMS
From the Life of A Woman

by Elean Thomas

Foreword by Dr. Carolyn Cooper
Introduction by Dr. Trevor Munroe

KARIA PRESS

Word Rythms
From the Life of A Woman

First published in 1986 by **Karia Press.**
Copyright © Elean Thomas, 1986.
Copyright © Foreword Dr. Carolyn Cooper
Department of English University of the West Indies
Mona, Jamaica.
Copyright © Introduction Dr. Trevor Munroe
General Secretary, Workers Party of Jamaica,
President, University & Allied Workers Union.

Cover design by Neil Ross.
Typeset by Karia.
Printed at Black Rose Press.

ISBN 0 946918 40 6 Pb.
ISBN 0 946918 41 4 Hb.

Karia Press
BCM Karia
London WC1N 3XX
United Kingdom

Dedication

For Louise
my mother
who always tries her best
against all odds
and who bequeaths me
a heritage of dignity and struggle
against all odds

For Uncle Natty
who first taught me to be proud of
my class, colour and sex
and who bequeaths me
a heritage of struggle

Contents

Acknowledgments
Give Thanks . . .
To:

Trevor, Linnette and all the other comrades of Workers Party of Jamaica who were my first audience and most consistent critics

Give Thanks

To:

Janice and the other sisters of the Committee of Women for Progress and their Women's Clubs who aided and abetted my efforts, first gave this work an audience in the communities of my country and were my first publisher.

Give Thanks

To:

My Father who first exposed me to the rhythms of our people through the Church

Give Thanks

To:

Mervyn Morris who took the time and effort to selflessly show me how to turn the creative key

Give Thanks

To:

Beverly Anderson-Manley, Daphne Kelly, Florizel O'Conner, Phyllis Green, Joan Ffrench, Carol Lawes, Arthur 'Sluggo' Newland, Basil Fairclough, Patrick Smikle, Brian Meeks, Rupert Lewis, Maureen Warner-Lewis, Phyllis Coard, Andaye, Essop Pahad, Meg Pahad, Miki Doyle, Junior 'Jo-Jo' Robinson (deceased) and Jacqueline Creft (deceased) who through the years and at different times, not only gave a listening ear and a critical eye but also spurred me on with their nagging question — *When are we going to read your works in a book?*

Give Thanks

To:

The Communist Party, Government and People of Czechoslovakia, the World Marxist Review Collective whose sacrifices, labour and goodwill provided the excellent conditions of life and work in Prague which greatly assisted the completion of this manuscript.

Give Thanks

To:

Marge who typed the manuscript
 A tedious labour of love

Give Thanks

To:

Desmond Johnson and Akira Press who organised my first reading among our people in England

Give Thanks

To:

Buzz Johnson, the other sisters and brothers of Karia Press and their associates who made the final output possible

Give Thanks

To:

The struggling people of Jamaica and the world who inspired this work.

Give Thanks

Foreword

Elean Thomas artfully describes her creative writing as "Word Rhythms from the lives of the common woman". Disclaiming the labels "muse", "scholar", "wise one" and "poet", which she considers to be pretentious, Elean distances herself from the "learned scholars" who may "criticize and sneer and laugh". She addresses an intimate audience with whom she shares a wide range of communal concerns:

> I live in the midst of my people. We work side by side. We struggle side by side. It is this, that conceives the ideas which I write about. Having written, I then ask my people — 'what do you think?' They are the final judge and jury. If they say its worthless, then maybe I try planting yams or making shoes. These activities are of unarguable social worth.

As a committed political activist, Elean often writes on issues that are overtly political, as in "Liberation Beat (To a South African Freedom Fighter)". In the poem "I Am" she defines herself, and her political mission, thus:

> I hate the system
> Which sucks our blood
> I will one day
> with my people
> Overthrow that system

I am a Black, African, Caribbean
Communist woman

As a woman, Elean is alert to the complex social and
political constraints that bind many women to a life of
drudgery. See, for example, "Litany of a Housewife". In
the scathingly satirical piece 'Ain't It A Shame", Elean
describes the complacency of both women and men,
who perpetuate the cycle of female dependency by their
very passivity:

> Aint it a shame
> That so many
> Still think it
> NATURAL
> For the Woman to go FIRST
> Yet remain LAST
>
> And aint it a shame
> That so many
> WOMEN
> Still agree

The short story "Josina" is an excellent example of
Elean's literary skill in portraying sensitive political
issues. The narrative documents the destruction of a
community of squatters by the "blue bag, blue stripe,
red stripe hurricane" of State authority. There are
sharp visual details, a clarity of political vision — a
chilling, sombre mood. The deceptive innocence of the
child's perspective, which Elean assumes in the tale, is
appropriately ironic. The young girl is overwhelmed by
the gratuitous violence of the predatory, male hurricane:

> My nine year old belly begin to tremble and
> thunder and scream with razor sharp pains

from left to right. (I learnt later that women feel things in our bellies). A rolling and a groaning began in my belly and moved upwards and downwards, filling my legs, my stomach, my chest, till it filled my ears and head and it was all around me.

But there are as well hopeful poems in which Elean affirms the mutually supportive affection between men and women. In "Love Song to a Special One", the lover asks:

> You stand by me
> I stand by you
>
> Could this be . . .
> Love?

Indeed, Elean's struggle for "women's liberation" is subsumed in the larger battle for "people's liberation". In "A Matter of Words" she distinguishes between "women's equality" and "women's liberation":

> Women's Equality
> Women's Liberation
> A matter of different words?
>
> Equality in poverty
> Equality in exploitation
> Equality in brutality
> Equality in class
>   and race
>   discrimination?

She concludes:

> People's Liberation
> A necessary

Inevitable
Human Reality

Thus Elean cautions her sisters in the poem "Make Sure", to curb their rapacious lust for things, lest they emasculate their men:

> MAKE SURE
> We
> WE
> ARE NOT
> Of those women
> Who suck the loins of our men
> BONE DRY
> AND LEAVE THEM
> DRY BONES
> in the valley.

The biblical allusion to Ezekiel's vision of the valley of dry bones introduces a note of tonal incongruity in a poem that is decidedly risque; but the weight of the Scriptures does reinforce the gravity of the problem — domestic prostitution. The commercial nature of exploitative sexual relationships is cleverly imaged thus:

> And for your price
> You demand
> AND TAKE
> HIS BALLS

> And store them safely away
> Along with the camphor balls
> Among the bedspreads pillowcases
> and towels

Elean Thomas' work is simply about freedom from

the weight of oppression — whatever form it assumes.
In flight, she engages our attention:

> We will never know
>   if we can fly
> Unless we break
>   those subtler chains
>   And soar
>   or fall.

Dr. Carolyn Cooper
Department of English
University of the West Indies Mona, Jamaica

Introduction

In her **TESTIMONIAL,** Elean Thomas describes
herself as just "a common woman". Those who read this
collection, and moreso those who have known Elean as I
have for over fifteen years, will immediately understand
that this description is at best only one-half the truth.
Elean is indeed also a very uncommon woman, and her
Word Rhythms is a very uncommon work. The fact is
that it is not yet common for an ordinary Jamaican to
become a communist, to have the courage of their
convictions and to declare openly under the Seaga-
Reagan government that this is where they stand. It is
even more uncommon for an ordinary Jamaican woman
to become communist than it is for an ordinary Jamaican man. Most of all, it is still too uncommon for the
Jamaican woman — communist or non-communist — to
consider her experience worthy, of anyone's attention,
to write of her experience, and to publish it for the
judgement of the working people.

Such things are uncommon because our people and,
most of all, our black women from the working class are
very much kept down, blocked by the system from
knowing themselves - what is for them, what is against
them; their achievements, their potential, their worth.
And therefore, only the uncommon consciousness, dog-
gedness and confidence of Elean could bring forth this
work at this time.

But, in another sense, Elean is right: she is but a
"common woman" — what she experiences, what she
sees, what she hears, what she feels in the rhythms of the

pages that follow is indeed common to the Jamaican woman — most of all to the black Jamaican woman from the "lower classes". In and through Elean's words, what is common is given uncommon expression and is viewed from the as yet uncommon, but increasingly supported perspective, of the Jamaican communist.

Which working woman under the Seaga-Reagan oppression will fail to see herself in *One Day In A Supermarket* — compelled by the prices under the second slavery "to check everything / one / by one / by one. . ."? How common it is for tens of thousands of women to be made into domestic slaves by the system, and too often by the man as well, to ". . . Cook and clean and wash / mountains of shirts / and pants / and nappies / and dresses / Then you / the man / say / I am only fit to do domestic work." And which Jamaican woman — capitalist, professional, middle class, peasant, worker, unemployed — does not have the experience of performing miracles of survival, or, despite starting from behind, performing equal to, sometimes better than the man — then to be denied equal recognition? To this, Elean says: "Ain't that a Shame" — and not just to the women but moreso to the man who, when it comes to the woman more often than not fails to give credit where credit is due.

In *Child Abuse,* Elean expresses the "kill-dead" pressure which is driving so many women to desperation in trying to bring up the children in conditions of near starvation.

> Ah might jus get off
> ah mi head today
> Because me and them can't go on
> Living so
> Miles upon miles of walking
> to find a job

        no job to be found
        One step-father after another
        To get some help
        No help to be gotten
        One boyfriend after another
        To have some love
        No love for me and them

But then, in all of this maddening frustration and oppression, Elean like the "common woman", finds time and need to wonder at the meaning of love, to speak of dance and the enjoyment of life; not to avoid struggle — but in the course of struggle for self-respect and liberation from oppression.

In these pages no man should believe that we have here only the common experiences of the woman. Of necessity, the man who reads, sees the all too common abuses by the man — communist man, revolutionary man, reformist, and most of all reactionary man — all as man, however powerless under imperialism, set in a position of privilege in respect of woman, and therefore in however small a way, beneficiary as well as victim of imperialism: The delinquent mate providing his woman with things but not with companionship — in Elean's verses as in life — wonders "what more could she want?" The delinquent father, the child abusing grandfather, the womaniser, giving the outside woman, *The Concubine*, the convenient line about the wife — Each comes to life in the "Word Paintings".

No man or woman can read this collection without understanding better the subjection of women, and without understanding the capacity of women to awaken, to struggle and to achieve — Moreso because this understanding is not passed on, as too often happens, in the form of some boring political article with slogans and cliches, but in lively verses and concrete

images which come even more true to life to those who
have heard Elean read these lines. Elean herself tells us
the road that she travelled, the road that more and more
women in our Party, in our country and in the world are
travelling and will be helped to travel by *Word Rhythms:*

> The first stage is
> Self-Awareness
> Other-Awareness
> Plan Awareness
>
> The second stage is
> Not-Afraidness
>
> The third stage is
> Standing-up
> Stepping-out
> Practical
> DOING-ness

With women like Elean, with the common and uncommon that she expresses about our "African Caribbean communist woman", the struggle may be set back,
even defeated, for a time, but never vanquished. In our
ultimate victory over oppression of woman and in the
ultimate liberation of our people, I am the more con-
fident having read Elean Thomas' work. Let us hope
that Elean will write more and not only her but other
revolutionary and communists artists as well will make
more time to learn from as well as to strengthen the
culture of the peoples struggle.

Dr. Trevor Munroe
General Secretary, Workers Party of Jamaica,
President, University & Allied Workers Union.

January, 1986.

Testimonial

In 1947 when the world was still struggling to recover from the ravishes of the Nazi-imposed War, I was beginning my struggle in a tiny village in the hills of St. Catherine, Caribbean island of Jamaica—to become a living breathing part of that world. That struggle was realised on the 18th day of September.

I am the result of the union between a quiet, dignified, brave working-class woman who works at anything which can provide a decent and honest living and a boppish, dashing middle-class Preacher-man.

Like most Black parents, the first thing they taught me was to seek after Education and Learning. The second thing was Respect Yourself as a Woman.

Taking Lesson one to heart, I went through Primary and Secondary (then called *High)* schools. Eventually reached University (of the West Indies)— considered the pinnacle for those who seek after Education and Learning. Studied Political Science and History there. Given a 'paper' saying 'Bachelor of Arts' for my efforts. It helped somewhat in increasing my 'marketability' as a Journalist and Publicist, which has been my profession for over fifteen years..

I have no certificate which records what I have learnt from just simply living and struggling. Yet that has been my most important, on-going School.

As to Lesson two, I cannot adequately judge. Because there are differing opinions as to what is proper for a Woman to say and do and live.

All I can say is, that I have tried to live, not on my

belly, my back or on my knees but standing upon my feet with my arms linked into those of my people.

And in living this way, it began to become more and more inconceivable to me that it could be right for so many bad things to happen to human persons simply because they were poor, or Black or born in one section of the world as against another or physically handicapped or looked different from others or spoke different from others. Or were old. Or were children. Or were sellers of labour instead of buyers of labour. Or because they were born Woman.

Came that point in time when I stopped trying to understand it and paid most attention to working with others of like mind to change it. And that is how and why I became a Communist and an activist of the Workers Party of Jamaica.

There is not a separation between the brain, the hand, the feet. They are not in contradiction with each other. That is how I see my profession, my political activity and my attempts at creative writing.

I live in the midst of my people. We work side by side. We struggle side by side. It is this, that conceives the ideas which I write about. Having written, I then ask my people—*what do you think*? They are the final judge and jury. If they say its worthless, then maybe I try planting yams or making shoes. These activities are of unarguable social worth.

I have had such interaction in Readings in the urban communities of my own country, Jamaica. In my Region, in Barbados and Grenada. On the other side of the world, in Czechoslovakia and in the German Democratic Republic.

The Committee of Women for Progress of Jamaica was my first Publisher—putting my *Ode To Woman* on their 1983 greeting card for International Women's Day. *Focus* Publishers took a particular liking to *What More Could She Want* and have included it in their 1984

Anthology of works of Jamaican poets and writers.

I call my pieces *Word-Rhythms*. I honestly believe it is pretentious to call them 'poems'. They are merely word-sketches, word-photographs, word-drawings, word-paintings, word-beats—WORD RHYTHMS FROM THE LIFE OF A COMMON WOMAN.

Word Rhythms From The Lives of the Common Woman

i am no muse
no scholar
no wise one
no poet

i cannot
turn a rhyme
   a metre
   a phrase

i am but one
of tens of millions of
ordinary and common persons
THE COMMON WOMAN
YET NOT COMMON TO ALL

Who see and feel and live
   THE WORLD
through the bare opaque window
and in the midst of
The beating hot Sun
The drowning Rain
The blasting Winds
The unexpected joys
   of Sunshine
or tender MOON
Cooling Breezes
Of the Space inhabited
   by ordinary Common Persons
and in particular
The COMMON WOMAN

And from what I see
and feel and live
Together with others
I try to make
Word Photographs
Word Drawings
WORD PAINTINGS
WORD BEATS
WORD Rhythms
from the lives
of the COMMON WOMAN.

LOOKING GLASS

Come here
I am going to tell you
a secret
About how to look
into a woman's soul

Look here
You see these things
They come in different shapes
and sizes
Different shades
and colours

You think you know
them well
You think you know
their various uses
But
Listen here
Did you know
They are a looking glass
into a woman's soul

When the soul is enchain-ed
When the pressure builds up
When life in babylon-system
Is slowly crushing out
life itself

They hang their heads
they become bloodless
they shrink-in upon themselves

A Matter of Words?

Women's Equality
Women's Liberation
A matter of different words?

Equality in poverty
Equality in exploitation
Equality in brutality
Equality in class
    and race
    discrimination?

       OR

Liberation from poverty
Liberation from exploitation
Liberation from brutality
Liberation from class
    race and sex
    discrimination?

    Women's Equality
    Women's Liberation
A matter of different words?

       OR

Peoples' Liberation
    A necessary

    Inevitable
    Human Reality

Love Song:
One of These Days

One of these days
We will cover each other
with rich juice
    of sweetness
    Babies' oil
    pouring slowly
    over pulsing bodies
What a pity
    if that day never
      comes

Dialectics of Struggle

The first stage is
        Self-Awareness
Other-Awareness
Plain Awareness

The second stage is
        Not-Afraidness

The third stage is
        Standing-up
        Stepping-out
            Practical
        DOING-ness

The first stage
must be conceived
Must issue forth
        Before
the second can be born
or the third conceived

But stages are conceived
        Born
        Co-exist
        Develop
        Thrive together
Towards a fullness
of struggle

Josina

I met Josina when I was nine years old. To this day, I never knew how old she was. The day Josina came, I was washing dishes in the two pudding pans—one with water to wash, the other with water to rinse—in the kitchen. We, my mother, step-father and I, occupied the main front room of a three-room house. In the room at the back lived a Sugar Factory worker and his woman who took in washing. In the other room—the one opening to the side of the front verandah—lived the landlord (white Jamaican whose branch of the family had fallen from grace with their peers some time between slavery and colonialism and by now mainly drank rum and collected rent. He was also into the business of molesting little girls).

On our side of the road, there was the barber (called *Barber)* and his always-sick wife Miss Maude (people said that a girlfriend of his had obeahed her but I later came to understand that she suffered from the common female problem of Fibroids); the respectable dress-maker, Miss Pat, married to the Prison Warder—and further down the road, the Browns—people who had lived on that same street, in that same house, in that same town for three generations and who were beginning to be doctors and civil servants before my people were even off the plantation.

My mother worked at the Textile Factory and my step-father at the Sugar Factory. The abysmal illusions of workers who are close to the petit-bourgeoisie! The working class on the road aspired to be like the

dressmaker, Miss Pat and her husband, the Prison
Warder. Miss Pat and her husband, the Prison Warder,
aspired to be like the Browns. And the Browns? They
aspired to be what they were three generations ago
before there was all this *indiscipline* with Rastas and
Trade Unions and Political Parties and so on.

So that on my side of the road, its residents preferred
to pretend that the other side of the road was not there.
For on the other side of the road, was the Hangman's
Cemetary, abandoned some years before but with the
gravestones standing out among the tall stunted grass;
perhaps to remind especially those on my side of the
road where you would end up if you were not decent and
mixed with only decent people.

If you walk alongside the cemetary, on the main road,
just as you pass the train gate there is a wide track. On
the left of this track, is a clearing, through which you can
walk to get on to the trainline, or crossing the trainline,
into the belly of the cemetary. On the other side is a gully
which borders the clearing. Turning neither right nor
left, after you have come off the main road into the
clearing, but going straight, you come into Tawes Pen—
a dirt poor community of minute farmers, self-employed
artisans, manual workers and perpetually unemployed.
Children on our side of the road were reared from birth
to view anything or anyone on the other side of the road
as a specie of human being not quite human and
certainly not decent. But it was from Tawes Pen that the
Jonkonoo Band came every Christmas so even the most
well -behaved children from my side of the road had, at
one time or the other, ignored our parent's instructions
not to mix with the Tawes Pen people.

I was telling you however about the day I met Josina
for the first time. I was washing the dishes at about
eleven in the morning during the holiday times when I
heard a lot of excitement coming from over the other
side of the road. I ran over there and saw that the activity

was in the clearing. I saw some Rastas—about 10 men, one woman and two children, setting up a settlement in the clearing on the cemetary land.

It was one year after the *General Elections* which brought the *Self-Government Party* to power. More importantly, it was four years after the Marxist-Socialists had been expelled from that Party and many of the leaders hounded off the island. It was also after the all our prominent statesmen and politicians had agreed with the British that the best thing for the island was to model our self-government system on that of our colonial benefactors who had taught us so much for nearly 400 years. Of course, many of the workers either did not know of this consensus or were too ignorant to grasp its meaning. Because they continued to strike for better pay and conditions of work. Many of the unemployed continued to demand jobs. Many ruined farmers continued to migrate to the city and demand places to live. Some of all these joined Rastafari and increased their chants against *Babylon System.* The response of the authorities was terrible bulldozing of communities, mass arrests and evictions.

These people in the clearing had been evicted and like others of them, where there were no relatives to *kotch* with, no way else out, they *captured* land. These had *captured* a part of the Hangman's Cemetary.

They soon had up two shelters—a large one for the men, a smaller one for the woman and children. I stood along with other curious men, women and children as the newcomers set up residence and was there again in the evening when they started to drum and chant.

I used to steal away over there in the days, when mainly the woman, her children and the unemployed men were there. The men who had jobs worked on construction sites but most of them were either unemployed *hustlers* or sellers of some small thing— broom or bottles (in those days, sweeties and cigarettes were not such popular items of higglery as they are now). I used to steal away there in the nights also, when my parents were on night shift at the factory.

I had naturally noticed Josina on that first day but I came to know her and her children—one baby on breast, one toddler—better later on.

Josina had thick, black, coarse plaits, usually four or five sticking from her head, dark eyes, high forehead topping an oval face which was flat in front with African nose and black lips. Medium breasts (already *dropped* from being the only steady source of nutrient for the children), rounded belly, a high behind and strong legs coming down to small ankles and feet. Just above the left ankle was the lasting deep scar of an ulcer which had taken gallons of hot water and Dettol, tons of Blue Stone and two years out of school before anyone could be sure she wouldn't lose the leg.

Josina didn't talk very much. She was one of those women—seen so often among our working people—who long ago decided that it took too much out of you to both talk and fight life—so just decided to fight life—quietly. With no one to leave the children with, looking for a job did not make much sense, even if there was any to find— for her. She stayed in the settlement, sewed, made things with her hands like crude wooden and stuffed toys for the children, tidied the place, cooked some- times, washed and lived from day to day.

We would sit in the clearing on many a day, Josina and I. She doing something and watching the children, me trying to find out about their lives—how did they come there, where would they go from there. She never spoke about the children's father—whom he was, what had happened to him, why was he not there with her and the children. The extent of her life that she was willing to bare was—she was a woman with two children who had nowhere to live and lived in that place at that moment. In terms of the men among whom she lived, she was everybody's woman—yet she was nobody's woman.

One evening when I went over there, they were quarrelling. One of their numbers had tried to crash Josina's hut in the night and to force her submission to him. She had fought him off successfully and had raised it in the Council (the evening drumming and chanting). He sought to defend his action by saying it was a matter between Josina and himself. Class struggle raged between those who supported him in this and those who held onto—*this woman among us for us to protect her and her children; why should we seek to defile her just because she need our protection.* These won out—one main reason being that the leader of the community, the highly respected Elder, carried this position firmly and would not back down.

I was at home alone again the day they came to root out Josina, her children and her brethren. They came in one jeep and one Black Mariah—blue seams and red seams (the Khaki must have stayed in the office).

Josina was there along with the children. They came like a hurricane—blue bag, blue stripe, red stripe hurricane. Quick as a flash, Josina grabbed up the children—one into her arms, the toddler in her skirts between her legs.

They started in with batons, with sledgehammers, with tearing hands, with stomping feet. They tore down the little shelter over the fireside, made up of sticks, crocus bags and old zinc. When that was down, they hammered the aluminum pot. They kicked the Dutch Pot into the gully. They wouldn't even let the firestones remain but threw them into the gully too.

They tore down the two sleeping huts; they kicked the few meagre items of clothing into the dirt and the rubble.

And Josina just stood there, among the curious onlookers, watching the hurricane.

By this time some of the resident men had begun to

drift to the scene one by one, word must have gotten to them. They helped to swell the crowd of on-lookers, mainly from Tawes Pen. No one dared pierce the eye of the blue seam and red seam hurricane.

I had never before in my nine years seen such a scene of total violence.

When the police had beaten, thrashed and torn down everything. When the cardboard, the cellotex, the bits of board, the zinc, which had made up the huts, lay flat and scattered in the dust. When every last *grip*, suitcase, carton box containing their life's collections, had been mashed and crushed and flashed out in the dirt and into the gully, like hungry beasts unsated, they kicked the dirt and looked around for more things to destroy. And prayed that one or more of the people forming a half-ring on the sidelines, would intervene, so they could mash and crush some people too.

And then they saw Josina's pail. In those days every woman had a pail. My mother had a pail. I would soon have a pail. You soaked and washed your *small clothes* in the pail until they were so white and glistening on the clothes line, it hurt your eyes to look directly at them hanging in the sun.

Josina's pail was some way away from the settlement, behind a big cotton tree. The pail was neatly covered with a clean piece of cardboard weighted down by a stone.

At the same time they saw the pail, Josina remember-ed the paid. Putting the baby on the dirt, disentangling the toddler from between her legs, she started forward to rescue the pail. They reached it before she did. And one of the policemen kicked the pail high in the clearing. Bloody water and small clothes flew all around the clearing, the small clothes seeming to fly up and up and up—and then to come down and down and down—for an eternity—before settling plop, plop, plop, in the dirt.

For one moment, Josina and every man, woman and child, including some of the policemen themselves, stood together on the edge of the world. There was a thunderous silence, then an extended collective gasp—in the midst of which Josina walked to the middle of the clearing and began, as in a trance, to gather the small clothes from the dirt.

My nine year old belly began to tremble and thunder and roll and scream with razor sharp pains from left to right (I learnt later that women feel things in our bellies). A rolling and groaning began in my belly and moved upwards and downwards, filling my legs, my stomach, my chest, till it filled my ears and head and it was all around me. And then I realised that the murmuring and rumbling were also coming from the 100 or so men, women and children gathered there. It started as a low murmur and then it rose like the mighty wave of a sea in the throes of a tidal wave beginning. Like a hurricane coming out of the gulf of Mexico and gathering force and fury.

And the Elder (the one who had defended Josina) brought out from the depths of his guts a terrible roar—*Babylon . . . Fall*!! The crowd picked up the ominous chant—*Babylon you must, you must fall down, Babylon you must fall down*... The chant followed me all the way over to my side of the street as I ran home. I never saw Josina again but for years her face was to remain with me as she stood in the clearing, the small clothes covered with dirt in her hands.

Nature's Factory

Living in tropical climes
 all her life
  where
 continuous sunshine
  alternates
with greyish-opaque rain
to bring into being
  but two seasons

  She really was surprised
to see that in Autumn
in four-season places
Trees do
  in fact
Convert and transform
the normal green
of their leaves
    Into

Pure golds
Riotous yellows
Pinky oranges
Cool reds
Hot reds
Just
Reds
Purples
and all the different shades of brown
with ever-changing tones

 Today
all yellows and purples

Tomorrow
flecked with browns and gold
   The Next Day
a wonderful glorious all-colour
         mix

Like one top-producing
   Dye factory
with millions of workers
On 24-hour shifts
Ever-working to adorn
     the space
from Earth
    To Sky.

Concubine's Lament

You say
You have not loved her
For at least the last ten years

Then why
is she the wife
and I the concubine

You say
you have not slept together
Since your teenaged son was six

Then why is she
   the wife
And I
the concubine

You say
That when you're with me
There's nothing else you could desire

Then why is she the wife
And I the concubine

You say
That for all your life
You've been looking for a woman
Exactly like I am

Then why is she
the wife
   and I
The Concubine

42

As years
and years
roll by

I begin
      to understand
it matters not
how little you love her
or how much you love me

If we're both with you
until we're old
and hair and teeth fall out

She will still remain
      the wife
      and I
      the Concubine

To A Delinquent Father

I don't matter much
   Things
You don't give me
or can't give me

Because I know
You don't have
   Things

I just want
if i have any problem
if there's some little thing
that's worrying me mind
I can sit down with you
   and talk it over

Surely That
You can give

I don't matter much
   Things
You dont give me
Or can't give me

Because I know
You don't have
   Things

I just want you to be
   my Father

Surely That
   You can give.

Rasta Warrior

I
am
a
Dark-skinned
Thick-lipped
Female
Negro
Rastafarian

Six months from now
I will be
a
Dark-skinned
Thick-lipped
Female
Pregnant
Negro Rastafarian

And I am going
to fight them
For the Present
And future

Of me
Me husband
And me pickney them
I am going to fight them

Indira

I saw you once
in living breathing
reality
but i have known you well
all my life

Because whenever
i looked up
i could always see you
towering there
beautiful and graceful
feminine and warm
tall and strong
and tough and firm

A WOMAN STANDING UPON HER FEET

Your voice would swell
and rise and spread out
as the waters covering the earth
at high tide
Demanding freedom from War
from hunger
from shame
for the small and poor
of all the world
No iron lady you
but

A WOMAN STANDING UPON HER FEET

No easy burden

you bore responsibility
for millions
you bore
the weight of a continent
intensely coveted
by those who make slaves
of others

Yet your shoulders
never slumped
you were always

A WOMAN STANDING UPON HER FEET

You gave birth and suckled
children of your nation
you did not bow down
in paralysing grief
when fruits of your womb
were trampled underfoot

What unwelcome germ
was it
what disease-carrying virus
in woman's love
or high-brow pride
which made you clasp the scorpion
so closely to your breast
Did you hope
to wean it
from its wicked intentions
its inglorious mission
with nourishing mother's milk

Did you learn
in the brief seconds
of glaring awareness
as its poisonous sting
was speeding towards
your heart

Did you learn
that mother's milk
fed to the scorpion
only makes its sting
more deadly

i see your body lying
without a breath
in the front room
of your great father's house

your body is enfolded
in the flag of your country
which you held so high

your body is garlanded
with the flowers of the love
of your peoples
whom you led
so fearlessly

But crouch-ed leering
in a backroom of the house
in which room you helped
to put and keep him
Crouch-ed leering
Eyes and Feet fixed
towards the front room
Crouch-ed leering
Crocodile tears
running great streaks
and cracks
upon his actor's mask
Crouch-ed leering
IS THE VERY ONE
who fed and nurtured
THE SCORPION
you clasped so closely
to your breast

If your people keep him confined
to the backroom
If your people
eventually kick your murderer
and his fork-ed tongue condolences
completely out the house

What more fitting tribute
to INDIRA
Towering and beautiful
graceful and feminine
tall and strong
and tough and firm

A WOMAN STANDING UPON HER FEET

Space

She has made a space
　　Inside herself
Where she goes alone sometimes

No renting storms
No wracking tensions
can enter this space
　　Inside herself
Unless she takes them there
And that she never does
She's made a stress-free space

Sometimes she goes there alone
　　　with a memory
Sometimes with a good book
Sometimes with her thoughts
Sometimes just with herself
To this space she's made
　　Inside herself

If she goes there too frequently
or stays there too long
She knows she's losing her balance
With the space
Outside herself

But without this space she's made
Inside herself
Where she goes alone sometimes
She would be hopelessly lost in the space
Outside herself.

Child Abuse I
(Under This-ya Pressure-ya)

A feel like a going to get off
        a me head today
A must get off
        a me head today

I did think yesterday was bad
        But today

I can't even find the sugar
        to mix the water
Nor the strength to walk
        and go line up
        to catch the water

When the pickney-them make
        even the slightest little sound
Me whole body tense-up
A feel like a would-a lick
        them down
And stamp-up me foot all over them

I will never born another pickney again

Whole night last night
Me lay down stiff-out
        pon me belly
Me lock me teeth
and me jaw and me lip-them
        Tight-tight
To prevent the bitter hungry bile
        from come up out of the stomach

When the little two-year-old one
Crawl-up pon him knee
And touch me soft-soft
    pon me side
A feel like a could-a mash out
    him brains
and scatter him all over the floor

I will never born another pickney again

A might just get off
    a me head today
Because me and them can't go on
    living so
Miles upon miles of walking
    to find a job
  No job to be found
One step-father after another
    to get some help
  No help to be gotten
One boyfriend after another
    to have some love
  No love for me and them

I will never born another pickney again

A may as well get off
    a me head today
Then somebody who can afford
    to have them
Might take them . . .

The little two-year-old one
A creep-up quiet-quiet
    pon me again
Him close close to me now
    him-a twine him little wingy
      finger them
    into me skirt-tail
    Him hold him head down
    but him looking up

Straight-up into me soul
Him lean him head
Pon the bottom of me hungry belly

Him just lean him head there
And looking straight-up into
      me soul . . .

A can't get off a me head today
No way A can get off
      a me head today

I have to find the way out

But under this-ya pressure-ya

I will never born another pickney again.

I Am

I am an African woman
I am a Black Caribbean Woman
      I work
      I eat
      I struggle
      I sleep
      I wake up
  I laugh, I dance, I cry
      I love
      I give birth

I am a Communist woman
      I work
      I eat
      I struggle
      I sleep
      I wake up
  I laugh, I dance, I cry
      I give birth
      I love
      I love my people

      I hate the system
      which sucks our blood
      I will one day
      with my people
      Overthrow that system
I am a Black, African, Caribbean
      Communist woman

Love Song To A Special One

I have never seen
      felt
   nor heard
in every language under the sun
  a word more us-ed
     and abus-ed
       than
      Love

I have never seen
      felt
   nor heard
in every language under the sun
A word more us-ed
    Yet more misunderstood
    More mystified
      than
      Love

I can never hope
    to unravel
all the millions of yards
    of threads
Of this mystery
   of Love

So I tentatively
    pull
      one stitch

And it is
that

In good times
  or in bad
In ups
  or downs
  or levels
  In joy

  or sadness
In nearness
  or in distance

In acceptance
  or rejection

In objective
or subjective
      conditions

You stand by me
    I stand by you

    Could this be . . .
      Love?

I have never seen
      felt
  nor heard
in every language under the sun
  a word more us-ed
  yet more mystified
      than
        love

Notes to Bob Marley

Bob-man

Last night I dreamed again of your tough, wise little leonine face looking deep-deep into my soul as we reasoned one with the other about Rastafari, Haile Mariam Mengistu, Ethiopia's new dawning, blandishments of the fled Crown Prince.

RASTA NO WORK FOR NO CIA

Bob-man,

Last night I stood again among a million of our people — yours and mine — in the streets of our island — workers, farmers, artistes, youth, women, children — gathered to say goodbye — to your body, nourishing your spirit with our love. I saw again those who persecuted you and yours but yesterday now uttering fine eulogies from their vulturine cavities.

HYPROCRITES AND PARASITES WILL COME UP AND TAKE A BITE . . .

Bob-man,

Last night again I saw your taut little body — stiff

with the wounds of the enemy's bullets — poised against the canvass of the blue-black tropical midnight skies over our Park of National Heroes — Smile Jamaica Concert. I was standing again among hundreds of thousands waiting patiently to hear if the terrorist had silenced your sound. You raised a cry through your wounded throat and the sound was loud and clear.

GET UP STAND UP STAND UP FOR YOUR RIGHTS

Bob-man,

Last night again I saw you in Zimbabwe. Your left hand raised, forefinger pointed — accusing, beseeching, appealing, encouraging — from the strength of your loins, the urgent summons issuing . . .

WE'VE BEEN TRODDING ON YOUR WINE-PRESS MUCH TOO LONG

REBEL
RE—BE—E—E—EELL!

Bob-man,

Today I see South Africans answering your summons.

CAUSE NONE-A-THEM CAN STOP THE TIME

Liberation Beat
(To a South African Freedom Fighter)

Moving through the bushes
Your AK in your hands
Surrounded by your people
Your heart and theirs
      Beat

Boom di di Boom
Boom di di Boom
Boom di di Boom
A BEAT OF LIBERATION
Moving through the gold mines
A pamphlet in your hands
Surrounded by the workers
Your pulse and theirs
      Throb

Boom di di Boom
Boom di di Boom
Boom di di Boom
A BEAT OF LIBERATION
Moving through the schoolrooms
Black history on your lips
Surrounded by the students
Your hands and theirs
      Clap

Boom di di Boom
Boom di di Boom
Boom di di Boom
A BEAT OF LIBERATION
Moving through the prisons
Conviction in your head

Surrounded by the prisoners
Your blood and theirs
      Surge

Boom di di Boom
Boom di di Boom
Boom di di Boom

A BEAT OF LIBERATION

Moving through the Bantustans
Freedom Charter round your loins
Surrounded by the women
Your feet and theirs
      March

Boom di di Boom
Boom di di Boom
Boom di di Boom
A BEAT OF LIBERATION

       The Merchant
       in his stock-ed vault
       Sorting out your diamonds

       Than Banker
       in Fort Knox
       Stacking up your gold

       The Racist
       in his palace
       Calling up his armies

       When
From far and near
Above and below
To the right
To the left
And All Around
Your people's feet are upon them

Stomping
Stomping
Stomping
Boom di di Boom
Boom di di Boom
Boom di di Boom
Boom di di Boom
Boom di di Boom
Boom – THE BEAT OF LIBERATION

What If . . .?

(Thoughts on the Middle East Situation)

Tens of millions of Black people
        perished
in the Middle Passage

Tens of millions of Black people
        perished
on sugar cane and cotton plantations
in the not-so-New World.

Tens of millions of Black people
        Have no traditions
    We can call our own
    Boxed-about
    from continent to continent
            Country to Country
        Permanent asimilados

    What if . . .
Black people owned
        many powerful financial institutions

    What if
Black people had the power
        to make mighty kings and presidents
            take note

    What if
The great Western powers
felt guilty about
the African diaspora

        What if
These powers carved out a section

of Africa
And said to Black people
in the West
Take this and build a mighty
State.

What if
Black people of the diaspora
With this powerful backing
Took the best parts
of Africa

Could there really be any peace
With our brothers and sisters
who had remained behind?
Is there a better formula
for setting brother against
brother
sister against sister?

What More Could She Want

What a wicked dreadful and unreasonable woman!
        Look pon me foot
        The minibus wheel
            Run right over
            The middle of me instep
            Before me coulda squint
            It swell up big big
        like jackfruit pon me
            You dont know is what happen?

        Is that damn wicked woman at me house
        Is she pray God for me
        Why the minibus wheel
            Run right over
        The middle of me instep

    She always a pray for bad things
            to happen to me
    She always a follow follow me
            up and down
            with her complaining
    Just because me wont stay
            in the house with her
            at night-time

    She know that me have to hustle
            in the day-time
    Me no must have the night
            for meself?

    Drink me rum
            play domino

with me friend them
and do me other
Little business them

She is me woman yes!
but she is old time thing
me no must have
another little young thing
to rub up me jaw
And make me feel young and sprucy
What a wicked dreadful and unreasonable woman, eh

Me take good care of her
she tell me that she getting
a hard time on her job
me tell her to leave it
And come home and sit down

Me rent a little shop
me stock it out full
me put her into it
me tell her
that anything she sell
Is for she and the children them.

She have food to eat
she have clothes to wear
I give her house to live in
She dont have to leave the house
For nothing at all
not even to go to a show
Because me give her a T.V. too
What a wicked dreadful and unreasonable woman

One time
when me never
visit her
for about
two weeks
You should a hear how she bawl
and carry on!

Say me not treating her like human being
    say she lonely
    Say she need me company

    Is what she talking bout, eh?
      She dont have
      the shop
      to work into
She dont have
      the house
      to keep clean
She dont have
      dirty clothes
      to wash and iron
She dont have
      two children
      to take care of
      and to talk to

    What more could she want?
What a wicked dreadful and unreasonable woman, eh?

Litany of A Housewife

I stay in this house
    from morn till night
And cook and clean and wash
  Mountains of shirts
    and pants
    and nappies
    and dresses
       Then you say
      I am only fit to do domestic work

I stay in this house
    from morn till night
And kitchy-kitchy coo
     da da
     ma ma
  With the children
  Then you wonder
Why I only talk baby-talk

I stay in this house
    from morn till night
And share all the gossip
    and woes
with my sister across the fence
    who stays in that house
      from morn till night
Then you ask
Why do I nag and gossip so

I stay in this house
    from morn till night
      Oblivious

of national production targets
foreign exchange deficits
neutron death
MX missiles
Star wars at the door

American boots of death
Over new-born Nicaragua
Ten million feet
One hundred million hearts
Beating for peace and life
Multi-coloured hordes of
mankind shouting yes to
Social Revolution.

Social Revolution
which alone
can free me
from staying in this house
from morn till night
And the making of which
is demanding
demanding
demanding
That I no longer stay
in this house
from morn till night

One Day in A Supermarket

Me have to check
        Everything
            One
            By one
            By one

No way me can spend
        The same money
        That me spend last month
        This month

Or we bound fe land up
        Out a door
        When me can't pay the rent

We bound fe plunge into darkness
        When them cut off the light

Me corn and bunion bound fe rebel
        Or me drop down dead
        With tiredness
When me have fe walk it
        Go a work this month

Food
    Is still
    The most
    Important though

But
    Me have to check everything
    One
    By one

By one

No salt fish
   No salt mackerel
   No bully beef
   No milk powder

Only five pound pack
   A flour
   and sugar
At evergreen prices
   Two little soup bone
   Batter with dry season
One wingy chicken

What you say cashier
   God almighty
One hundred and thirtyfive dollars!
   And more cheeng!
   Cheeng! Cheeng!
Going up and up
Pon de Cash Register

Staap
   But this thing serious!

To A Fighting Man-Son

Across a crowded conference floor
Our messages merged
We may never see each other
       Again
       But
       I
   Just wanted you to know
       that
on that day
my heart touched yours
And the blood flowed
      warmly
   Between both hearts
   You must have felt it too
    Fighting Man-son?

Class Struggle I : Reciprocal Classroom

You taught me how
    to stand upon my feet
And be a different type of woman

You taught me love
        Rejection
And how to cope with rejection
As a different type of woman
Standing upon my feet

You taught me order
    Discipline
    Denial of self

What did I teach you
        Tell me
I must have taught you
            something

I can teach you how to feel
    and read
A look, a smile, a frown
I can teach you how to feel
With all of your body
And all of your senses
    Natural vibrations
    Of a bang-belly
    Skull-forehead
            Child
    Screw-face
    Eyes gleaming out
    With sure intelligence
        of a cruel system

     doomed!

I can teach you how to touch
   Without touching
the agony of a man too physically
        weak
to help his woman lift the pan
   of water up the stairs

I can teach you how to open
     your very being
to the sun, the trees, the breeze
    to suck the sun
  into all of you
Till it starts a laugh
  in the seat of your belly
And spill it through
  wide-open mouth

I can teach you
  How to dance Reggae.

Dance This Dance

I don't want to ever stop
   Dancing
With my Body

Le me ever Dance this Dance

When the drums start-up
the Bass-guitar
tender saxaphone
poignant flute
piercing trombone
Electric reaches the Brain
   BAM

Let me ever Dance this Dance

The Head cannot keep still
Shoulders must move
You think the Trunk
is going to be
out of line?

Let me ever Dance this Dance

By which time the Feet
are on the slow rhythmic-march
the Backside has to pump
to the beat of the Heart
in tune with the Bass-guitar

Let met ever Dance this Dance

The Blood must race

to keep up with the Drums
Reaches the Crotch
Shimmering musky sweaty
Heat
Rhythm wild
Rhythm wild
Body wild
Body wild

Let me ever Dance this Dance

The day I stop
    Dancing
With my Body
I am no more
of my people

The day I stop
    Dancing
With my Body
I am dead.

The Fashion Show

The Ballroom of the Exclusivets Hi-Price International Hotel is a fairy-land scene of tinkling music, soft lighting and muted tones.

The Emcee in well-trained, finishing-school modulated tones — chimes:

Ladies and gentlemen, welcome to the Premiere Fashion Event of the year: The Exclusivets Fall Showing.

At $500 per person (for charity), you can eat all the mouth-watering gourmet delights your stomach can hold. You can drink all the golden and sparkling diamond liquor your blood can dilute.

The slim beautiful models are twirling round and round on stage — lovely, polished, flawless creatures.

In the distinguished audience, the woman gape and ooh! and aah! at the clothes.

The men gape and aargh! and aargh! at the models. The Sportwear Line is complete. The last of the Executive working Girl Line is on stage. After the intermission (and by which time the buyers will have reached a suitably mellow stage of drunkeness) will come the top-price Deluxe Line. The last trim, fashionably efficient Executive Working Girl disappears from the stage. Lights go down on stage . . . up in the audience. Music swells. Whiskey and champagne flow. Satisfied laughter rises. The sound and feel of good times are unmistakable.

But backstage, the Manageress of the Fashion Show is pacing up and down. Wringing her hands and foaming at the mouth. The No. one model has just burst into tears — despite the pleas from the other girls that this will surely ruin her face!

Horror of horrors! The Fashion Show is to begin again in half-an-hour and the Star Garment — the foundation-piece of the Exclusivets Fall Line — has not yet come from the factory.

A driver races out of the car-park of the Exclusivets Hi-Price International Hotel at ninety miles an hour.

Destination: Low-Bite District . . . on the Waterfront.

In Low-Bite District, most of the factories and shops are silent and shuttered. In the nearby Shanty-Town, ghost-like figures move around in the dim, flickering light of kerosene lamps or by wood fires, preparing the evening meal.

A little boy of ten years is at the door of one of the better shacks.

He warns his smaller sisters:
'Lock the door!
Don't let nobody in
Don't play with the lamp
Don't come out of the house
till I come back.'

He walks through the foot-made track. Crosses over Low-Bite Highway and arrives at the gate of Exclusivets Hi-Fashion Factory (For Export Only).

'Guardie, you see me mudder come out yet?' — he asks the aged watchman.

"No, me son, she working nuff overtime fe oono. Them have on a big Fashion Show at some Hotel and the woman-them been working night and day. Them pay envelope should-a fat this week."

Inside the factory, the *mudder* is thinking the same thing as bent over a low counter, she is putting the finishing hand-stitches on the Star Garment.

Stitch — *one dollar a hour for the Sports Line and
    Working Girl line*
Stitch — *a whole two dollar a hour for the Deluxe Line*
Stitch — *time and a half for overtime*

Stitch — *five hours overtime this evening and one extra
    hour if them pay me for me lunch time and breaktime
    that me work through.*
Stitch — *then Supervisor Bulldoze promise me a bonus
    of 50 cents a hour if a finish this dress by 8.00
    o'clock*
Stitch — *should-a can buy school uniform for even one
    of the pickney them this week*
Stitch — *Burp! A should-a did eat something today,
    but I couldn't stop.*
Stitch — *Burp! Lawd, the gas a ride me chest!
    Burp!*
Stitch — *Keep near to me, me Jesus. Just make a finish
    them couple stitches here.*
Stitch — *Maybe if a stop little and drink some water
    — me can't remember if I did bring any peppermint
    with me today.*
Stitch — *Lawd, Supervisor Bulldoze coming! A bet is
    the dress she coming for.*
Stitch — *Only 3 more stitch left, maam. Yes, maam,
    you know you can depend on me. The dress will
    ready in time, maam.*
Sti . . . .

The pain gave her a massive kick in the chest. She
folded over the low counter . . . . she and the Star
Garment beginning to slide slowly to the factory floor.

The other women rush from their machines towards
her. but Supervisor Bulldoze reaches her first . . . . and
rescues the Star Garment.

'Is a good thing is only 2 stitch did leave. Them won't
notice it. Come one a oonu, take this to the Presser,

them waiting on it at the Fashion Show.'

The little ten-year old boy is inside the factory gates by the Guard House.

'Guardie, you sure me mudder in there? She should-a come out already.'

"You dont hear a tell you she working overtime for the big Fashion Show. Dont bother me again, just wait, she soon come out."

Ah, a woman is coming out. She has a long parcel in her hand. But no work bag. His mother always carry her work bag with her. The woman is going to a car. No .... is not his mother.

Is:

'MISS MAE, MISS MAE, YOU SEE ME MUD-DER, YOU SEE ME MUDDER?'

In the Ballroom of the Exclusivets Hi-Price International Hotel is a fairy-land scene of tinkling music, soft lighting and muted tones.

On stage, the curtain rises on the Deluxe Line. The Star Garment, the foundation piece of the Exclusivets Fall Showing is about to appear. The hush is so tangible, the excitement so great, the patrons are afraid even to breathe. The stage is dark. Then the lights go up .... focussed just on stage.

And the slimmest, the most beautiful, the highest-priced model, bears Star Garment on stage.

The hush is broken with a gasp! As the model twirls and twirls yards and yards of the most unbelievably delicate, intricate hand-embroidered overlay in all the colours under the sun — on black satin. The lighting catches the colours. It is too beautiful to bear. Exclusivets has done it again! Every woman in that room would kill to have Star Garment, every man to have it enfolded around his woman's body.

The Emcee's voice rises above her usual well-trained, finishing school, modulated tones.

This is a dress fit only for a queen. Exclusivets, your top fashion house, decided not to put a price on it but to take sealed bids.

The buyers and husbands are tumbling over each other, the whiskey and champagne glasses . . . to get backstage.

THE FASHION SHOW IS OVER.

Ode To Woman

For being
    Mother
    Wife
    Daughter
    Sister
    Grandmother
WORKER
For being WOMAN
  For all the times you have
     stood up
  While some are falling
  For all the love you give
You are of the foundation
  of our future.

Soldier Of Fortune

Yesterday they sent you to Grenada
        to kill and maim
People just like you

Your Mama is a-wondering
Just where you are

The-Day-Before they sent you to Vietnam
        with orders to burn
Gooks on sight

Your Mama is a-wondering
Don't you know we are Gooks too

Today they are sending you to Nicaragua
        to create mayhem
And Destruction

Your Mama is a-wondering
Just when you'll learn.

Child Abuse II

When I was seven years old
Seventy-year-old nice family friend
Mr. Smith brought me sweeties
and my very first real doll

My mother and my father
    my uncles and my aunties
    laughed and roared
        at my delight
As i danced round and round
    with happiness

And then after dinner
as we sat on the verandah
nice seventy-year-old family friend
    Mr. Smith held me
        and bumped me on his lap

My mother and father
My uncles and my aunties
    laughed and roared
As I bumped up and down
On Mr. Smith's lap
I gritted my teeth
    and asked myself
Should I be feeling pain
Whenever nice Mr. Smith
Bumped me down
    upon his lap?

When I was eight years old
seventy-one-year-old nice family friend
Mr. Smith still liked to bump

me on his lap

Would my mother and my father
My uncles and my aunties
Still laugh and roar
if I should show them
the blood running down
    my legs?

Until Women Learn

Until women learn
To make it
With each other
We will never be able
To make it
With men

When you can't eat
Can't sleep
Can't work
Can't think
Except about him
Then you know
You ain't learnt yet

When you allow him
To play you off
Against your sisters
To spend all your time
Planning and plotting
And scheming
How to hold him
Then you know
You ain't learnt yet

When you spend all your time
fighting tooth and nail
To carve him out
As your own little piece
Of Property
And nothing else is reality
Then you know
You ain't learnt yet

When there is not a view
A belief in the world
You hold independent
Of him
When you are prepared
To stay in the back
Because his ego
Can't take you
Standing beside him
And you see no cause
For struggle in this
Then you know
You ain't learnt yet

When you can't
Independently feel
The fulfillment of
Socially useful work
Well done
Can't feel
the burning beauty
Of our islands' sun
On hills of bananas
Chocolate coconut mango
Morning Glory
Bouganvillas
Rice and Peas Bush
Black and white sea sand
Among your toes
Our people
Black and Brown
And yearning to be free
Can't feel all these things
Unless he walks beside you
Then you know
You ain't learnt yet

When you are prepared
To make fundamental concessions
Running dead counter
To all your principles

And beliefs held dear
Because
'You just don't wanna be lonely'
Then you know
You ain't learnt yet

Today is the best day
To begin to learn

For Until women learn
To make it
With each other
We will never
Be able
To really make it
With men.

Fact is / April Fool

Nina of the Caucusus
small and pretty
dainty and neat
Voice like an ever-so-quiet
bubbling mountain stream
Eyelids fluttering
over large wide eyes
in deceptive shyness
At the handsome swaggering
know-it-all visitor

All smirk and snicker
sneer and leer
He tries to order
her around
Telling her loud and clear
Your rightful place
is still behind me
And don't you go forgetting

Nina of the Caucusus
just smiles
her shy little smile
And then begins
to speak

> Fact Is
Nina of the Caucusus
Is the Manager
of a Six-thousand-acre
Tea Farm

Fact Is
Nina of the Caucusus
Is responsible
to her people
to her country
For the welfare
   Well-being
And production
of thousands of workers

Fact Is
Nina's Tea Farm
is among the pride and joy
of her nation
Contributes
   its full share
   to the gross national product

Fact Is
What Nina doesn't know
about Farm Management
and Tea growing
Is not yet known to many

Fact Is
There are tens of thousands
   of Ninas here
And another being born
   every minute

Fact Is
He who tries to keep
the Ninas behind
Is who cannot see
   these facts

Fact Is
He who cannot see
   these facts
Is who has been left
            Behind

Like an April Fool.

Fetter

You can talk to me boyfriend
      for me maam?

A beg you
Please talk to me boyfriend
      for me maam

Him beat me
Nearly kill me
Last night

Just because
Him wouldn't believe me
When I tell him that
I was on the picket line
for all the time
of the Strike

Him say is another man
   I was with

And him beat me
Nearly kill me
Last night.

Those Subtler Chains
(Class Struggle II)

I say I want to write a book
        about women
You say better to concentrate
        on gathering information
    about how other people
    have dealt with the question
            of women

I say
Am I not a woman
Have I not been gathering
            information
about women
    all my life
Have I not been
        Living information
about women
    all my life

So tell me
Why shouldn't I write a book
        about women
        Right NOW?

If I didn't know you better
        I'd say
This is just another example
of keeping subtle chains
    around my feet
Damming my intellect
    Pruning my growth
But knowing you
        As I do

I know
     it
     is
     that
You are afraid
Afraid that the book
   Will not be a mistress-piece
You are afraid
   that learned scholars
   will criticize and sneer and laugh

Well damn the learned scholars
I want to write a book
     about women
I been living information
     about women
   all my life
As to the learned scholars
   they may have past
   their time of learning
What matters that
I am not so much concerned
   about them
I am more concerned
That you should really learn
We cannot come into the fullness
     of our heritage
Unless in action
With our own hands
We together tear down the walls
    of our own self-doubt
Even should we be crushed to pieces
   in the effort
Or suffocate in the dust
    from the torn-down walls

We will never know
   if we can fly
Unless we break
   those subtler chains
     And soar
       or fall.

Aint It A Shame

I squat in the wet icy ditch
    Beside you
my weapon cocked at the target's throat
the cold creeping up
under the legs of my baggy army pants
    for hours
Until my clit is like a chip of ice
my womb a frozen ball

Still we must wait
the right moment is everything now

    At last
It is the moment
The situation demands that I go
    in front
We advance

Within minutes its all over
Mission Number Nineteen successfully completed

    AND THEN

In your half-yearly Report to the High Command
you just happen to put more emphasis on the
One Mission that I missed
confined to camp with terrible period pains
You have on your wisest, most understanding look,
as you conclude:

'Our women soldiers perform valiantly
but they have so many, SPECIAL problems,
it would be a bit unrealistic to expect them to be able

to meet the demands of being in our Officer Ranks.'

NOW AINT THAT A SHAME

When I am eight-months pregnant
with Maria
The police Special Squad
descend like locusts
on our innocent community
Bullets flying
Boots a-crashing-in doors
Gunbutts stomping stomping

I cover the mouths of the two little ones
and pull them quietly underneath
the house

Then I cradle my eight-month belly
tightly in my arms
And facing the raging beasts in the yard
I look straight into the depths of their unfeeling
Gun-muzzle eyes

And say:
'He is not here
I have not seen him in months'
And prayed they wouldn't look
or worse still
Shoot
Behind my grandmother's old wardrobe

AND THEN

When I tell you I have signed up to become a Member
of the Movement
You have on your most betray-ed look, as you say:

'But you can't manage that, Love.
Who going to take care of the house and see that no
harm come to the children while you gone to meetings
and marches?'

NOW AINT THAT A SHAME

I am up before the sun has even said
Good morning
I make your breakfast
get the children ready for school
make the sandwiches for your lunch
tidy the house
Get myself ready
Walk to the bus-stop
hang half-way out of the door of the minibus
    all the way

Punch the factory clock at 7.00 a.m.
    sharp
Stand the whole time on the production line
Give up the little overtime money
to leave at 3.00 p.m.

At 4.00 o'clock I am in the solidarity march
with the striking Bauxite Workers
By 6.00 my feet's one big bunion
surrounded by a field of corns
But I stay some more to hear
your stirring speech
about equality and rights for all
Its such a good speech
I clap and clap
until the blood is purple
under the skin of my palms

AND THEN

At home I get your pan of water and baking soda so you
can soak your weary feet.
I rub balm on your aching back and mix gargle
for your parch-ed throat
The children need someone to help them with their
homework and they're kicking up a stink. You have on
your most long-suffering look as you ask:

'Dinner not ready yet? Tomorrow is another early
day, you know.'

NOW AINT THAT A SHAME

I share your joy when
that speech we wrote together
is appaulded to the skies

That time they put you in the jail
and I had to run the organisation
    until you were free
I glowed and blushed
my heart swelled up and beat
like an amplified time bomb
when you looked at me and said
    Well Done

AND THEN

I was elected to the Executive.I became one of the
Managing Directors and Chairperson of
a major Committee

BUT

    One year later
You cannot look me in the face,
when i insist and you deny
That all I've done is taken minutes, type letters
and be a sounding-board for the other
Menaging Directors

NOW AINT THAT A SHAME

All those years
you have been out of work
When every single thing we need
to go on living
have doubled trebled quadripuled
    in price
I have become an economic acrobat

Performing debt-defying feats

The time I organised and administered
   the Disaster Fund
Raising three million dollars
making sure all needs were met
putting aside funds for contingencies
We ended up with a saving
of a quarter million dollars
Through stringent budgetary controls

AND THEN

At the meeting to decide the new Cabinet,
you have on your most insightful look as you say:

'We really need a highly qualified and experienced
MAN for the Ministry of Finance.'

NOW AINT THAT A SHAME

Aint it a shame
That so many
Still think it
   NATURAL
For the Woman to go FIRST
Yet remain LAST

And aint it a shame
That so many
 WOMEN
Still agree
ITS NATURAL

NOW — Aint THAT
A SHAME?

Of Colours . . . And Countries

White is not a colour
It is an attitude
A certain behaviour

Black is not a colour
    It is a statement
    of a shared past
    a present reality
    a future intent

Africa is not a threat
It is the cradle of mankind
A conscience ever-pricking
the souls of the human race
to do what's right

The Middle Passage
    was not a luxury cruise
It was the gas-chambers
    for the African peoples

Africa is not just a continent
It is a condition of determined
            struggle
for what must be

Africa is humble brave Vietnam
    Sacrificing generations
        to be free

Africa is tough little Nicaragua
    Struggling to survive

Africa is Ethiopia
  Fighting to control
    even the elements

Russia is Africa
  Triumphant.

International Telephone Blues

Hello
Operator?
I'd like to make a call
to Kingston
Jamaica

Where?

Kingston Jamaica

Did you say
India?

No operator
KINGSTON
Jamaica

In India?

Operator
Can't you understand
My child is sick
and me Mom needs help
I got to call home
In the WEST INDIES
NOT the EAST INDIES

Oh!
Jamaica

Yes operator
That's what I been saying
For all of the time

Hold a moment please

   Hello
   This is me
   How are things
   A-going there

   Hello madam
Are you getting through
   On your call
   To India?

Operator I did not call India

   O-Kay
   go ahead

   Hello
Are you still there
   What
   Dying?
Why are you shouting so
Why are you whispering so

   Maam?
Are you speaking
With your party?

   Yes Yes Yes

   Hello
did you say
   Dying?

Oh Crying!
With relief

So my child's O-Kay
And me Mom's got help
There's been another price rise
And another demo

O-Kay
Take care
Write soon

Hello
Operator?
Could you give me
the cost of my call
to Kingston
Jamaica

Madam
Only two hundred pounds
for calling all of the way
to India

Operator I did not call India

Hang up
I'll ring you back

Hello
Is your number
Europe 3241067?

Yes
Hold for your call

Operator
Who is calling?

Calcutta
India

But I did not call India

Hello
Is that Europe?
Calcutta India calling

But I dont know anyone
in Calcutta
India

Hello
Operator?
What the *** bamboozle
going on

I did not call India

Sorry Maam
There's been a mistake
You can hang up now
Everything's alright

Hello
Is this the Manager?
Yes Madam
What can I do for you?

Well
For a start
I would like to know
How my bill could be
five hundred pounds
When my phone's been off
for nearly a goddamn month.

One moment please
Madam
It's ever so easy to check

Oh we're so very happy
to clear up your query
without a minute's
waste of time

Our computors show
That in the week
When your phone was on

You made two long calls
To Calutta
India.

Unequal B's

When two men
whose spirit blend
Meet each other
they clasp
   hug
and rock
each other's body
Momentarily forget
their womenfolk
revel in the pure delight
of each other's company

Bystanders glow
smile indulgently
and call them a word
beginning with a
        B
How good to see
  such good
    Buddies!

When two women
whose spirit blend
Meet each other
  clasp
    hug
and rock
each other's body
Momentarily forget
their menfolk
revel in the pure delight
  of each other's company

104

Some bystanders glower
smirk suggestively
Call them a word
beginning with a
        B
And it is Not
        Buddies.

Don't Leave Me Behind

Don't leave me
    Behind
I am of you
and you are of me

Don't leave me
    Behind
Let us come together
  in all things

Because I am of you
And you are of me
I cannot reach the mountain-top
    unless you take me
And you cannot reach
    the mountain-top
Unless I take you.

Comparisons

In the city of Havana
   Cuba
You can find beauty parlours
Where you can be primped
  and polished and preened
For next-to-nothing pesos

In the city of Kingston
   Jamaica
You can find beauty parlours
Where you can be primped
  and polished and preened
For your whole month's pay

In the city of Havana
   Cuba
You cannot find
 a Charm School
Where you can be taught
the proper way to walk
and talk and pose
and model

In the city of Kingston
   Jamaica
You can find many
 Charm Schools
Where you are taught
the proper way to walk
talk, pose, model
and marry

In the city of Havana
       Cuba
You can find seven hospitals
for women's illnesses only
Specialists
on breasts, lumps, womb
and a hundred causes
of vaginal discharges

In the city of Kingston
       Jamaica
You can find two public general
    hospitals
Many American-funded
Birth-control clinics
    For a pain in the head
    they give you
    a coil in the womb
    to ease it
If you go to the clinic
for a rash on your leg
    they give you
    Dipo pro vera*.

*Long-acting contraceptive injection
prohibited from use in most developed countries

Make Sure

```
MAKE SURE
   WE
  ARE NOT
Of those women
Who suck the loins of our men
     BONE DRY
  AND—LEAVE THEM
   DRY BONES
   in the valley.
```

dish out your love and affection
to the exact measure
that he can shell out
Big house
Showroom furniture
Jewellery
Expensive things
and property
For the children's sake
        You say

Deprived of rights
and power
over your own destiny
Under the exploitative system
You immerse youself
in washing and cooking and cleaning
Day in
Day out

Yourself oppressed
You oppress other women

Keeping the household help
In your house till all hours of night
Day in
Day out

Keeping His house
Spic and Span
Looking Pretty
Entertaining his friends
Day in Day out

And for your price
You demand
    AND TAKE
    HIS BALLS

And store them safely away
Along with the camphor balls
Among the bedspreads pillowcases
    and towels

Make sure
That we are not
Of those women
Who suck the loins
    of our men
    Bone Dry
And leave them Dry Bones
    in the valley.

You watch him
Drink his life away
And you get him another bottle
    You watch him
Submerge his brain
Under constant clouds
of mind-killing drugs
And you buy him some more

    You watch him
Laze his hopes away
    or crawl

When he should stand and fight
And you caress
   his sensitive spots
You whisper in his ears
Don't worry baby
   I love you
   I will always be here
   to take care of you
   No need to worry
You prefer him this way
Because this way
You are sure to have him
      Helpless
to yourself alone

     Make Sure
That we are not of those women
     who suck
the loins of our men
     Bone Dry
And leave them
Dry Bones in the Valley

You smother and over-mother
   your man-child
Giving him no room
To develop
As an independent social being
To make up for the fact
that his father is not there
And to make the man-child fill
the void
Of your own aloneness

You are prepared to take
   all his decisions
     for him

From behind his back
And then you curse him
for not being a man

You
Call him a mampala man
if he tries to wash
and clean and cook
in your clean kitchen
And then you tie an old rag
round your head
and complain
how overburdened you are

        Make sure
We are not
        of those women
Who suck the loins of our men
    Bone Dry
and leave them Dry Bones
in the Valley

Sometimes he takes the step
    to liberate himself
To fully involve himself
in the struggle
for the liberation
of our people
    You
seek to pull him away
To Miami
To New York
To defending private property
and the class
that lives off private property

And then
when all of your million and one little wiles
    have failed
You look at him
And you say.

It's me
or the struggle

Make Sure
Make Sure my sisters
That we are not
of those women
Who suck the loins of our men
    Bone Dry
And leave them dry bones
In the valley.